UNIVERSITY OF TERAMO "G. D'Annunzio"

FACULTY OF LAW

CHAIR OF GENERAL THEORY OF LAW

Giacinto Auriti

The INTERNATIONAL REGULATION of MONETARY SYSTEM

Teramo 1996

"To say that a State can not pursue its goals due to lack of money is like saying that an engineer can not build roads for lack of miles".

INTRODUCTION

The investigation that we have proposed, as well as closing a gap in the doctrine of international law, has the novelty of a research on monetary science carried out by a lawyer rather than an economist. In order to prevent the prosecution of superficiality or invasion of a field investigation of other discipline, like to clarify that it is not possible to explain the structure, function, and therefore the very essence of the monetary instrument, without moving considerations strictly legal.

As it is known, the definitions proposed so far on money can be traced all to the two cases of "credit value and "conventional value". Since, both the credit that the convention are legal cases, it is obvious that it escapes to scientific scrutiny of the economist any possibility of a thorough analysis of the case. If one adds to this that the money is manifested in that particular form for which the symbol is considered to be "legal tender", we realizes that the establishment and the legal relevance that the currency symbol adopts with his social conscience mean that the monetary value objectify as well by virtue of a creative process that is exclusively legal. It is only later that the economist may want to consider this as well and evaluate protagonist of great importance in economic affairs.

Where never accept as a starting point of the monetary investigation the legal phenomenal from which money originates, its investigation would be seen as pure empirical fact because, lacking in it an awareness of the principles, it would lose the ability to realise cognitive processes of scientific dignity.

The prominence assumes that the clarification of the legal premises, the analysis of the processes and structures to creative moment of the money is accompanied, will be demonstrated in this investigation. Do not be surprised the reader of the new "scandalous" that might emerge from this research, because, once the demonstration highlighted the assumption is made, Viconian convinced of the principle of *verum et bonum convertuntur*, also would add *oportet ut scandala eveniant*.

Giacinto Auriti

TABLE OF CONTENTS

Chapter I
Analysis of the structures in international monetary
1. Evolution of the international monetary system
2. The Bretton Woods
3. The International Monetary Fund
4. The crisis of the international monetary system
5. The Gold Pool
6. The end of the Bretton Woods regime and the advent of the Dollar Standard
7. The special drawing rights (SDRs)
8. Critical considerations and comparison of the various types of international monetary policy
9. Rigidity and flexibility of monetary changes
10. The Multinational companies

Chapter II
Value and structure of the currency
11. Introductory explanations on the concept of value
12. Analysis of the various species of value judgements. The induced value of money
13. The rarity monetary
14. Money as a tool of social law. Monetary reform, labour costs
15. Credit worthiness and value (conventional) monetary
16. Relevance of form and legal institutionalization in the creation of the monetary value
17. Brief overview of the historical evolution of monetary symbols that cost nothing
18. Features monetary form and its implications on monetary regimes

Chapter III
Principles and guidelines for a reform of the monetary system
19. The futility of the money supply
20. The rarity money as a tool of domination
21. Recent developments in international monetary policy
22. Organic society and subjectivity instrumental. The SO-CALLED inverted pyramid
23. The uniform tax law as an instrument of the international monetary system
24. The heavy money as an instrument of monetary policy
25. Lines for a reform of the monetary system

Chapter I

ANALYSIS OF INTERNATIONAL MONETARY STRUCTURES

1. Evolution of the international monetary system.

The international monetary system is certainly the most important part of international law, because it affects not only economic aspects legally relevant for the international law, but considers also categories of interest of such importance, which can not be ignored in the interpretation of the same historical events of all time. The survey that we have proposed - albeit at an institutional level - fills a gap in the traditional teaching of international law. Worth in fact of being in the right place the fact that in the monetary system has been creating a new form of monetary sovereignty which is not only international, but also - in many respects - *supranational*.

The monetary regime, which traditionally was right on the strict principle of national sovereignty in a vision essentially isolationist, in fact, came to change its entirety in the period following the last world conflict.

Changing economic structures, with the most advanced technologies, came to greatly accelerate the
processes for production of wealth, and the impressive growth in traffic, which put in touch different worlds, markets and contractors of different nationalities and operating in different currency areas, letting perceive the need to link into a single monetary flows to these phenomena that accompany it.

This means meet the need to establish certain parameters for the determination of the monetary values, even expressed in different currencies, namely to establish a common denominator of the various currencies. The gold, which had traditionally performing this task, it was no longer sufficient to meet the ever increasing need for monetary liquidity. It required, therefore, the need to create a new instrument capable of fulfilling the function of international currency. The achievement of this purpose characterized the evolution of the new international system.

2. The Bretton Woods Agreement

From the period immediately following the last World War, there has been a substantial change on traditional monetary systems, in such a way as to make them particularly relevant for the international jurisprudence, and it would alter the political and economic balance of markets.

This new system has its origin in the Bretton Woods Agreement on 22nd July 1944. The work of this conference were based on the two projects presented respectively by Harry White, delegate of the United States, and John Maynard Keynes, British delegate, simultaneously published on 6th April 1943. Since around these two projects moved the conference and, as we shall see, the arguments and insights contained in them were widely enhancement in later developments of the international monetary system, make it here deserves a quick nod[1].

The White project - which was based on the realization of the International Monetary Fund - provided a so-called international stabilization fund for an extend not less than $ 5 billion, made up by contributions in gold and currencies of the participating countries.

To this fund could draw the member countries to meet their liquidity monetary needs[2]. It was provided for this purpose the creation of a monetary unit called *Unitas*, which would have had just as reserves these values.

White in fact considered the *Unitas* - with a gold content of 137 and 1/7 grains (equal to $ 10 of the time) – as international currency designed in the same way as a kind of representative credit of the values placed at his warranty. In this scheme the gold assumed a position of all relief and also in consideration of the fact that in that time the U.S. was the nation with the largest gold reserves.

According to the White plan, member states were obliged to yield to the Fund in exchange for their respective national currencies, all foreign currencies and gold, which they had come to have in excess compared with the quantity possessed at the time of their adherence to the Fund.

The White plan - which then was broadly welcomed in the creation of the International Monetary Fund - worked as a bank, in which each country appeared as "account holder" using traditional monetary foreign exchange (Gold and the respective currency). The project then was submitted to the limits of growth of the money supply that could not be proportionate to the need of money, ie the increase of economic development, but to the amount of the reserve.

The White project, which gave the appearance of a more reliable because it is based on a gold guarantee, in effect showed no serious expectation that there would be no arbitrary excesses in the issue of currency, as it had to demonstrate the subsequent development of monetary policy.

Also the Keynes project provided for the establishment of a new international monetary unit to be used as reserve: the *Bancor*, which, however, differed from the American, why did not precede the establishment of a fund of reserves as a condition of its issuance, as the *Bancor* was conceived purely as an international currency conventional, recognized as part of a currency union between states.

For the Keynes plan, the Clearing Union would have to function as a tool for transformation in Bancor of the equity assets of creditor countries. In the Keynes plan, therefore, the *Bancor* came to constitute a new money to be issued - on the assumption of a balance - in favour of the creditor country.

The Bancor should have the quality of units of measure of value, but not that to be the object of the value. We know that this is a hypothesis impossible, as it is not conceivable that a unit of measurement without the characteristic corresponding to that of the object to be measured. It would be like designing a kilogram that it had not the quality of the weight or a meter without the quality of the length.

He captures this aspect of the problem Mr. Palladino, who defines the amount of Bancor due to each country creditor, such as "theoretical limit of shares that would work as a simple obstacle to the debtor nations and as a basis for action to correct any imbalances and structural pathological"[3].

Therefore, the Keynes project would not have materialized nothing but the restriction of the same monetary sovereignty of Member countries, namely in considering the *Bancor* as a parameter value which commensurates the monetary increases of every nation.

The White and Keynes projects, even though they had the apparent affinity, were then structured on two concepts and monetary philosophies completely antithetical.

Both plans contemplated, however, an international institution: respectively a "Fund" for White and a "Clearing International Unit" for Keynes, in order to achieve a common currency and the necessary discipline limitations on the monetary policies of member countries.

The inability to merge into a single project the two solutions, came from the fact that the fundamentals of the two plans moving on two antithetical conceptions of the monetary value: for White the currency had credit worthiness, ie title representative of the values of the reserve, for Keynes the currency had to be purely conventional, that is, free from any form of reserve, while constituting itself reserves for the various central banks.

Both projects realised then the partial purposes, while presenting defects of great importance for different aspects.

The work of the Bretton Woods Conference took place with the participation of 44 nations sent by the President of the United States Franklin Delano Roosevelt.

The presidency was assumed by the Secretary of the U.S. Treasury Morgenthau. The Congress came to the unanimous condemnation of the monetary regime before the last World War, highlighting the need for remove the restriction of the foreign exchange and foreign trade, encouraging international cooperation. In closing speech made by Lord Keynes, was emphasized that the conference had to be considered as the beginning a new experience unprecedented.

"We have accomplished here in Bretton Woods something more meaningful than what is stated in the Final". With these words of Keynes is closed after three weeks, namely 22 July 1944, the work of the Conference.

3. The International Monetary Fund

The Bretton Woods led to the establishment of an operational tool for the implementation of the goals indicated by the conference: the International Monetary Fund. The conflicting opinions on which to structure the Monetary Fund reflected antithetical formulas proposed respectively by White and Keynes. It prevailed the thesis of America. The IMF was structured as a joint stock company, and the agreement that established the Fund entered into force on 17 December 1946.

Participation in the capital, represented in dues paid by each country, and the amount of which was determined on the basis of the economic power of the member countries, it was also the basis for the distribution of votes. The share of each country was made up to 25 per cent of gold and 75 per cent of the national currency. In exchange for those contributions the Countries acquired the ability to obtain Rights of withdrawal, that is, they could buy foreign currency, which is necessary to settle their debts. Expiry of the period to which the right of withdrawal was subjected to, the country that had used it had to buy back their own currency or reserve currency, or the foreign currency that had previously purchased. The maximum use of DSPs could not exceed 200 percent of the share of each Membership, in national currency.

This project safeguarded a position of apparent equilibrium between the various nations, because the dollar was supported by collateral golden. The acceptance of the American system led to such a program, so there is noticed that the availability of gold and dollars (if the issue would have to be limited at the ratio of $ 35 per ounce of gold) would not have been enough to an adequate increase in international monetary liquidity, in accordance with these purposes provided for by art. 1 of the Statute of the Fund.[4]

In structuring the International Monetary Fund were not taken into consideration any currency unit of account, that is used only in the accounts between States (*Unitas* and *Bancor*), as it became the operating principle, common to both projects, to recognize the function of the gold reference parameter to allow that member States could pay off their debts in gold.

4. The crisis of the international monetary system

The abandonment of the English frame with a reserve currency (Bancor) different from the national ones put the U.S. in a position of special privilege. The Bretton Woods agreements were in fact designed in such a way as to be violated with impunity, because no nation was placed in a position to control the breach, that is, check if the U.S. Treasury had issued dollars to a greater extent than allowed by the availability of gold reserves. Such control would in fact constituted an interference in the internal affairs of a foreign country does not permissible according to the principles of international law. This fundamental flaw of the Bretton Woods is nothing else, then, that the essential defect arising from misunderstanding of thinking about money as a title (credit) representative of the value of the reserve (golden or not) and not as purely conventional, which actually is.

This opportunity allowed to the U.S. in fact, the realization of a chronic deficit in its balance of payments. This is for the obvious reason that, unlike the member States, who were forced to drain the money in their markets to return to the IMF in terms of the borrowings, this problem did not arise for USA, whose deficit of balance of payments was pleased with the greatest of ease, as the U.S. Treasury, being the creator of the currency base of the system, it had no difficulty in providing.

This phenomenon caused the effect of a substantial imbalance in world markets, first of all because, as it was criticized mainly by France, with this system, the U.S. exported their inflation, and secondly place the bulk of imported goods and services caused a significant crisis in the American productive system, because this import market was prepared with the consequent slowdown in their production processes, unemployment and economic stagnation.

While most industrialized countries had to cope with inflationary pressures, on the other hand were benefit from a significant boost production, which was politically justified by the opportunity to rebuild economies distressed by the war. (The famous phrase of the well-known French economist Jacques Rueff, that "the U.S. returned to distribute pins to keep playing").
In fact, the dollar, going to invade monetary areas of other countries, came to deprive in the most essential of political sovereignty, because it has arrogated powers many of the monetary sovereignty of all the countries participating in the Monetary Fund. The rest of the system was structured in such a way that could not regardless of the use of the dollar as an international currency. From 1959 to 1971 all world markets were so overrun by masses of ever-increasing

dollars.

It begins at this point the phenomenon of Euro-dollar that technically are defined as dollars belonging to non-residents and causing a not light effect to determine non-monetary imbalances (abundance or scarcity of money) with displacements caused by speculative pressures from market to market.

The U.S., on the basis of the Bretton Woods and the establishment of the International Monetary Fund, they could enter the world markets of 10 billion dollars, but had virtually created gold-paper for 80 billion dollars. If, therefore, on the one hand the U.S. violated the monetary agreements, it was with the tacit consent of the majority of the central banks in the Western world, because it is inconceivable that the masses so significant of dollars could be put on world markets surreptitiously.

The antithesis which arose between the United States of America and the De Gaulle's France, particularly jealous of their monetary sovereignty, resulted, of course, in the request from the French side to convert in gold the masses of dollars within its own market. The French example was followed by other European banks, so that to keep faith convertibility at a ratio of $ 35 per troy ounce of gold, the United State of America from 1958 to 1971 suffered a copious spillage of gold for a total of approximately of 90,000 tons. The dollar began to weaken and the gold to take off again.

5. The Gold Pool

The prediction of the possibility of a rapid ebb of monetary value from paper to gold, which has always been a constant concern of the banking systems, because it threatens the same reliability and stability of the international monetary system[5], had prompted central banks to set up in 1961, in London, the Gold Pool in order to contain the price of the metal within the limits of $ 35 per troy ounce.

With this agreement, the banks were buying gold at a high price to sell it at a low price, this for the obvious reason that the loss incurred on the difference in value between the price of gold purchased and the price of gold sold, was abundantly rewarded by increases in the value obtained in the official prices of the currencies.

This control of the gold price, therefore, can not be understood if one considers that the banking system, having the ability to create nominal money at zero cost, and then when they have no limit and no cost for all the money that he needed, was more than offset the loss incurred in the sale of gold to underestimating the gold, making money on the corresponding and simultaneous increase in the purchasing power of the currency paper.

The overabundance of dollars in the market, however, caused such a large number of requests to convert dollars into gold, which in the last quarter of 1967 the reserves of the countries of the Western world, committed to supporting the dollar for the compliance with the terms of Bretton Woods, declined by $ 1,400 million, corresponding to about 1,250 tons of metal sold at a price of $ 35 per troy ounce. On 15 March 1968, the London market, unable to keep the face the ever-increasing demand for gold had to close, as well as the Zurich market. That of Paris, however, that had tied its monetary policy to gold, remained open and the price quickly rose from $ 35 to over 44 dollars an ounce. The event was of such resonance that the Governors of the central banks, which met after a few days in Washington decided to refrain from any form of intervention in the gold market.

In the statement released after the meeting was the following declaration: "The U.S. government will continue to buy and sell gold to the current price of $ 35 per ounce in transactions with the monetary authorities... The gold held by official bodies should only be used for transfers between monetary authorities. "

On this premise was constituted the double gold market: one reserved for transactions between central banks, in where the price of metal was kept rigidly to the level of $ 35 per ounce, the other of the free market, which the quotation was left floating according to the forces of supply and demand.

It should be noted that at that time the levitation of prices was also caused by the demands of particular importance made by space industries and electronic equipment for the construction of new building techniques. The result was the accentuation of the price difference of the two markets. This episode could cause significant effects also on the monetary system, because the debtor, that is, with the balance of payment deficit, were subjected to a further economic sacrifice to that of the accounts defined, because they are unable to pay with gold at free market prices; without saying that countries with substantial reserves of gold, including Italy, could see their limited potential to create new money, as it would have if the price of their gold reserves had been quoted freely.

With the imbalance that derived the monetary system was not the principle of exchange rate stability consecrated to Bretton Woods.

6. The end of the Bretton Woods regime and the advent of the Dollar Standard.

The tensions and discomfort where the U.S. Treasury came after the apparent impossibility of respecting the agreements Bretton Woods led to Nixon's historic declaration on 15th August 1971 in Camp David, with which it was announced the decision to suspend the convertibility of the dollar into gold.

Given the importance of this event, it seems appropriate to set out here the salient aspects of this new radical change in the monetary system internationally.

The American economy had been subjected to serious stress. The artificial overvaluation of the dollar compared to gold and then against other currencies currency, had opened the grave crisis in the U.S. market. The USA had paid a heavy price in terms of the economic crisis and productive brake in development for the achievement of dollar as the world reserve currency. It is not without significance that, at the same time not convertibility were announced by Nixon measures of tariff protection of 10 per cent on the price of goods imported from the United States.

The real justification why the U.S. came to this step based on the obvious consideration that, having been issued on international markets, SDRs (Special Drawing Rights) as a currency purely conventional[6] - that is, conceived without gold reserve - there was no reason that the dollar would continue to respect this constraint warranty.

Monetary theory sensed by Keynes in the design of Bancor had found its confirmation in the facts of history.

And even more this intuition had to be confirmed by the events that immediately followed the Nixon's declaration. It seemed in those days that the Western monetary system would collapse.

The fact that the dollar, at the opening of the foreign exchange market, it devalued for the minimum percentages against other currencies, it is evidence that the monetary value is purely conventional, whereas if it had been true the principle that the money was to be considered as faith deposit of gold or other reserves, the dollar would lose all its value. This means, in other words, that whatever the alchemy and the legal-political sophistry with which it is justified the value of money at the time of its issue, the fact remains essential that the currency derives value from fact that is accepted by the national communities purely and simply as a means of payment and as a measure of the value of real assets.

The U.S. had achieved international recognition for degrees that its currency, without reserve, was to be consider a reserve currency. It was the official transformation of the Gold Exchange Standard in the Dollar Standard.

It occurred in the days immediately following the Nixon's declaration an extraordinary meeting of European Ministers of economy in Brussels, after a lively discussion of solutions, in particular between France and Germany, it is ended with the decision that the dollar of the United States it is determined freely in certain countries of the Community with the free market exchange rate, whereas for others it was the establishment of a double market. On that occasion the Italian monetary authorities with a statement of the Treasury subsequently supplemented by a declaration of Foreign Exchange Office, declared free the lira to float against the dollar.

Along the same lines moved even the International Monetary Fund which, through a statement, made by Pierre Paul Schweitzer, Managing Director of the Fund, forwarded to the Ministers of Finance of the 118 member countries, put on guard against piecemeal solutions that would have seriously affected the results achieved in the period following the last world war. The implied meaning of this statement was essentially to propose the preservation of the dollar as a reserve currency. Moreover its abolition would have seriously harmed the interests of Countries that had treasured imposing masses of dollars, once downgraded from the rank of reserve money, would lose much of their value.

Significant occasion the expression used by Paul Samuelson: "The problem we face today is that of 80 billion dollars left on the stomach of the Central Banks."

7. The Special Drawing Rights (SDRs)

The monetary imbalances that had affected the stability of the dollar as the international reserve currency, induced the monetary authorities to plan a new instrument for international liquidity: the Special Drawing Rights (SDRs). The establishment of this new international reserve currency was approved by the Assembly of the central banks' governors of the member countries of the International Monetary Fund, held on 25-29 September 1967 in Rio De Janeiro. This new currency elaborate in its characteristics in four years of study by the "Club 10" (that is, the group of the ten most industrialized countries including Italy) was added to the other reserve currencies.

The value of the SDR was fixed on the basis of what $ 1, or 1/35 troy ounce of fine gold. This new monetary instrument had limited circulation transactions between States or between their central banks. With the establishment of **Special Drawing Rights** (which initially functioned as an instrument of deposits and credit facilities for exchange rates), the IMF became a central bank. We can say that was the realization that the Keynes project, which had foreseen the possibility of creating Bancor as a reserve currency purely conventional, regardless gold. According to the draft, the odds of Special Drawing Rights allocated to member countries were proportionate to the Shares in the International Monetary Fund. This feature was criticized because it produced the conservation of positions of privilege in favour of the economically stronger and blocked the possibility of development of economically weaker countries, which although they could achieve significant improvements economic and productive as long as they obtained the availability of the necessary financial means.

The Special Drawing Rights were regarded with great favour by most of the political and financial because it allowed the creation of monetary reserves without having to depend on the hegemony of the dollar, but in effects they had little practical significance because they came to represent just 3 percent of global reserves.

It should be noted, however, that the Special Drawing Rights are entered in the practice of international transactions for purposes other than those for which they were originally intended. American banks, Swiss, Swedish and French institutions public have issued securities denominated in Special Drawing Rights, or made SDRs deposits. The tolls for the transit through the Suez Canal were calculated in SDRs rather than in Egyptian pounds.

The possibility of the extension of their use has prompted the IMF to change the criteria for definition of the base value of the DSP and was replaced at the traditional reference (1/35 of an ounce of gold or a dollar) a so-called basket of 16 currencies, with effect from 1st July 1974; for "basket" meaning the average of monetary currencies. The currencies participating in the basket are those of the Member whose shares export of goods or services were higher than 1 per cent of world exports accounted for in the period 1968 - 72[7].

The preparation of this instrument, which was added to the traditional ones (the dollar and gold) was justified for the difficult situation in which the United States had come to see the impossibility of dollars in respect of the Bretton Woods agreements' issue.

8. Critical considerations and comparison of the various types of international monetary policy.

We can say - after the abolition of the Gold Exchange Standard and the establishment of the DSP - that gold has had its day and which is intended to be relegated to the role of simple commodity?
We do not believe this idea to be reliable for the following reasons.
Gold has the essential characteristics:
a) it set up by custom as the monetary value of a traditionally recognized in all Member States of the world;
b) it can not be producible *at nutum principis*;
c) it could not be demonetizable arbitrarily, because its value is conventionally and traditionally recognized before it by the States, by the same national communities;
d) it does not create problems of change, having already accepted as money, if not by all, by the vast majority of Member the world.

Moreover, the Achilles' heel of the DSP, as well as regulated in the international monetary system, lies in the fact of being currently considered in a monetary system hybrid, that is in which the monetary value is designed in part as conventional value and partly as credit worthiness. Upon issuance in fact the DSP is apart from the monetary reserve, so it has the conventional value, but instead is intended to be monetary reserves of various national currencies, which thus take credit worthiness representative of reserves.

If so, not at all unlikely that the DSP gradually become established as a reserve currency, we have ask whether banks respect the emission limit of their national currencies in proportion to the amount of DSP or other reserve currency in its availability.
I do not see why the various Member States of the IMF can not and should not follow the striking example given to the world by the United States of America, who have violated the emission limits agreed at Bretton Woods not only with impunity, making money, but also the big result to impose on the world the Dollar Standard.
To adopt the Keynesian system to replace gold with SDRs, does not change the fundamental peculiarity that an agreement of this type can be violated with impunity, because the issuance of the national currency, since - as we have detected - a prerogative of its own and exclusive of each state, does not allow interference or external controls adequate, without prejudice to the sovereignty itself.

This is the reason why, in spite of the sophisticated theories of the monetarists and the formal abolition of gold as a reserve, this metal continues to have considerable prestige in international transactions. Just consider for example that the OPEC countries (oil exporters) have pegged the value at a ratio of 20 barrels of oil per ounce troy of fine gold. (In the case that gold was devalued, it follows an automatic rebalancing, because countries oil buyers would have to pay in interest gold rather than dollars). To this must be added that the value of gold also derives from its utility to meet specific industrial needs of particular importance, especially in new highly sophisticated technologies.
For these reasons, the French economist Jacques Rueff claimed at the time of De Gaulle's government, the need for return to the gold standard pure, proposing the revaluation of the gold price of one hundred percent.
The real big change in the replacement of the *nominal money* with the *commodity money* is that, in *this* [commodity money as gold, NoT] the availability of the means necessary to the issue of money is in the hands of anyone who's got it, in a horizontal concept of the monetary function which remains the prerogative of the market, in *that* [nominal money, NoT] instead the monetary sovereignty is stand on a top-down concept, because it is in the hands of the issuing bank, which has statutory authority, as a monopoly to

issue currency without limit and without cost, arrogating, however, the ownership on an exclusive basis. In fact, the bank issues the currency and lending it, and because to lend money is the prerogative of the owner, it is by law (NoT: Continuing his research, Professor Auriti realized that, in fact, such a law that changes the ownership of the currency to the issuing bank does not exist. Lacking legal certainty regarding the first owner of the coin, it has been created a monetary structure that rests on the monetary empty and ignorance) declared owner of the money on the issue.

It is realised in this way the basic drawback of the current monetary system, in which those who create monetary values are the citizens, while those who appropriate it is the banking system that is on course to win over the monetary sovereignty, a supranational sovereignty, to say the world.
This reversal has developed a macroscopic indebtedness for all the peoples of the world with the banking system without counterpart. We must not forget, however, that the gold standard has not minor defects of allow the issue of money only to countries that have gold and consequently, to determine the increase of monetary liquidity not in proportion to the production needs and market, but to the amount of precious metal.
With the return to the gold standard would be the case, therefore, a drastic boost to deflationary monetary rarity with problems far greater than those of the system in nominal money. [Ndt: The Austrian School of Economics shows that, in a system where the ownership of the money is entrusted to the sovereignty of the people, deflation has instead effects positive. Like when, owning the shares, it sees the value go up over time]

This means that gold, while continuing to have its prestige, for the reasons stated above, in international relations between central banks, may not perform more than an auxiliary function and integrative system with paper money.
For these reasons, we should ask ourselves the daunting task of planning a reform of the international monetary system which has - as far as possible - the advantages of traditional systems without having the defects.

9. Rigidity and flexibility of monetary exchanges.

As part of the international monetary system, it is of particularly importance the exchange rate regime. This regime can not give stability and certainty of monetary values constituting the subject of international transactions, because the currency is a unit of measurement in the oscillating importance of its value, namely its purchasing power, not only for initiatives of monetary organs, but also for a variety of causes operating on the market (production, consumption, supply and demand for merchandise or money, oil prices, etc..), so it is not easy sometimes to identify the causes of the inflationary or deflationary push. Just think, for example, that the monetary inflation can be caused not only by abundance of money but also by increased demand for real assets [NoT: either by their scarcity]. The question, in fact, due to the price increase, which gives you a boost inflation can not be controlled by monetary authorities.

There are three exchange systems traditionally established:

a) free convertibility of currencies;
b) fixed exchange rate;
c) flexible exchange within strict limits of oscillation.

Each of these three systems has its strengths and weaknesses, of which deserves to give a few quick signs. To understand, even if in broad terms, this phenomenon, it is necessary to distinguish between *inflation* and *deflation*, which are monetary domestic phenomena, and *overestimation* and *underestimation*, which are international phenomena. Given the impossibility that the authorities check all monetary causes of the inflationary or deflationary push, to provide stability and reliance on estimates of the monetary value for the determination of prices in international sales (Imports and exports) was reached to plurilateral agreements for limiting the fluctuations of exchange rates between the various currencies within strict limits. On this line by the so-called "European monetary snake", which sets a limit fluctuations for European currencies to each other inside the snake, and outside against the U.S. dollar.

This tool, if it meets the needs of individual operators, as it gives a certain assurance on the maintenance of the exchange ratio, it is not without its drawbacks, because experience has shown to occur phenomena of artificial *overvaluation* or *undervaluation* of the currencies with damage of the balance of markets undergoing to fixed exchange rate regime rigid or semi-rigid.

As an example, we make the case that the initiation of the fixed exchange rate between the lira and the German mark in the ratio of 400 to 1. If at the time when the fixed exchange rate is adopted, a unit of goods costs 400 lire in Italy and 1 mark in Germany, the buyer will be indifferent to purchase the unit of goods in either country. If, however, despite the maintenance of a fixed exchange rate, domestic inflationary pressures are of different importance, and if inflation in Italy is 50 percent more and in Germany than of 0 per cent, is that the same unit of goods can be purchased in Italy at a price of 600 lira and Germany always at the same price of 1 mark. At this point the Italian economical operator will have an interest in buying that product in Germany, although under a fixed exchange rate will be put in a position to get 1 mark for 400 lire, paying at the old price the product in Germany.

This example means that with the fixed exchange rate is determined the arrangement of the market with a currency *overestimated* (in our example Italy) on import, with the consequent production downtime and economic stagnation, whereas the market with *undervalued* currency (in our example, Germany) is prepared the increase in production and for export.

These considerations highlight the fact that the change in the monetary exchange rates is far from neutral in the international exchange. And they learn how monetary instruments, which on one and incomplete view may appear adequate to eliminate some drawbacks (eg, exchange rate instability to other drawbacks is no less important than those who had loved one to delete).

For these reasons, monetary policy is oriented toward compromise formulas between the pattern of the stiffness and that of the freely floating exchange rates, in the format with rigid limits on the fluctuation large enough to avoid imposing phenomena of artificial monetary *overvaluation* or *undervaluation*.

10. The Multinational companies

On this basis we can explain the phenomenon of multinational corporations that have already established themselves as protagonists in all markets of the world. It is, as is well known, a joint stock company, or rather groups of corporation operating simultaneously on different markets in a position of absolute prominence. So much so that the phenomenon came to the attention of legislators as well as the doctrine and jurisprudence to contain the huge potential of conquering markets and disruptive competition.

The real reason for the increased vitality of these business groups lies in the fact that, being able to operate on markets of different countries and under different monetary systems, are in a position to take advantage of the favourable conjunctures for currency: for example by encouraging the production and export in countries with undervalued currency, and discouraging the production processes and promoting the import, in countries with overvalued currency. They are structured so that you can easily overcome the crisis caused by the reversal of the choice on monetary policy and foreign exchange, because they are in turn of the possibility of reversing their choices by encouraging or stopping the production processes in various markets.

Their economic power is therefore given by the fact that on their sails blow always the high winds of favourable ratio in currency exchanges, to which must be added the privilege of a limitless availability of funding.

It is obvious that this is possible because they are controlled by the same company that instrumentalise the monetary system.

As it has been rightly said, with multinational corporations, central banks act first on the market having available without cost and without limit all the money they want. And this is the real reason why the them there can be no attempt on the part of the normal competitive commercial enterprises.

The attempts so far proposed to stem the explosive action of these giants of the economy have remained inoperative and confined to the simple rank of good intentions, because the real problem is not so much to codify antitrust laws[8], as that ruling to reclaim the power of money to the banking system.

Notes to Chapter I:

[1] Of particular interest to note that the Bretton Woods Conference was preceded by a pre-conference, which attended by 15 States, it was held in Atlantic City, June 23rd to 30th, 1944. In addition to some procedural issues in that meeting were addressed in the preliminary aspects of great importance, such as the rules relating to exchange rate flexibility.

[2] The Fund's gold sales to the United States would be allowed to collect dollars, which even then was expected it should become the currency longer required to be normally used in international transactions. In this project so it was basically to bring the dollar as a reserve currency for other currencies, as anchored to a gold base.

[3] Giuseppe Palladino, "The U.S. economic recession," p. 129, ed. Signorelli, Rome 1958.

[4] Art. 1 of the Statute of the International Monetary Fund defines its purpose:
- To promote international monetary cooperation through a banking institution that allows for consultation and collaboration on international monetary problems;
- To facilitate the expansion and balanced growth of international trade, contributing in this way to promotion and preservation of high levels of employment and real income and to the development of resources for production of all member countries;
- Promote exchange stability, to maintain a correct ordering of the changes among the member countries, to avoid competitive devaluations;
- Eliminate exchange restrictions that hinder the development of international trade;
- Make available to member countries of the Fund's resources under appropriate conditions, to enable them to correct imbalances in their balance of payments without resorting to harmful measures of national or

International prosperity;
- Reduce the duration and lower the level of the deficit of the balance of payments of member countries.

[5] So that by 1694, the date of the founding of the Bank of England, the policy devaluing gold had resulted only a few revaluations of official small percentage, certainly not proportionate to the inflationary pressures of the market.

[6] See below par. 7.

[7] And that is: United States, Germany, England, France, Japan, Canada, Italy, Netherlands, Belgium, Sweden, Australia, Denmark, Norway, Spain, Austria, South Africa.

[8] See eg. the American anti-trust law and the Treaty of 1956 Articles. 85-90.

Chapter II

Value and structure of the currency

11. Introductory explanations on the concept of value.

The structuring of a fair international monetary system is a prerequisite for the normalization of political and economic equilibrium of the world. Since the theme, even if of fundamental importance, constitutes a purely technical aspect of economic policy, it must first be made clear that it presupposes an upstream speech that have to touch the essential aspects of rationality, ethics and cultural, because otherwise the monetary instrument goes crazy in the hands of who uses it, and it is no longer an instrument at the service of the community, but conversely a serious threat to their fundamental freedoms of the people.

When the terms breathtaking enter in the current language, the public loses awareness of their meaning and adapts to accept as normal even made absolutely extraordinary episodes. In fact, today's opinion public has accepted as quite normal and reasonable, the institutionalization of the so-called "paper gold".

To make a rational and objective evaluation of this phenomenon, it should be first noted that at the summit of international banking, it was possible to replace commodity money symbol because it has no monetary cost including a fundamental principle of the philosophy of value, namely, that the value is never a property of matter.

The solid, liquid, weight, volume, etc.. are the properties of matter, not the value, because it is always in a prediction, ie in a relationship between phases of time, which is a dimension of the spirit.

So for example we can say that a pen has value because we expect it to write. So the value is the relation between the time of the forecast and the expected time. Even the currency has value because everyone is willing to change goods against money because it expects to be able to give it against commodity currencies. Then the prediction of the conduct of itself, is the source of conventional monetary value. That said, we realize that even gold has value for money, not because it is gold, but because there was agreed that it has.

When you angle the attention of the general information about the convertibility of paper money in gold, in fact it should be noted as a necessary fact that instead it is pointless to give to the currency its purchasing power. The real reason why they want to keep the public illusion that the currency is a "faith of deposit" (receipt of deposit) and then pass off in the form of credit instrument a conventional value, is to induce the man in the street in the false conviction that there is an objective limit to the issuance of nominal money (as commensurate with the amount of reserves) and that the issue of the currency symbol from the bank can not be free – as instead it is - because it would be subject to the availability of real good "gold".

Under the pretext of gold reserve in the general opinion is essentially wishes to retain the conditioned reflex caused by ancient cultures based on the secular use of commodity-money, namely on a materialist conception of value. In this way, with the emission of paper currency structured as false bill or false faith of deposit, it induces the community to give commodity, which has a cost, against to gold-paper, which has no cost.

12. Analysis of the various species of value judgements.

In order to eliminate confusion between the various species of value judgements, within which also enter the value of money, we should use the expression of mathematical logic of the following hypothesis.

a) Act useful to the only operative subject

If we denote by t' the first phase (instrumental) of the value, with t'' the second phase (hedonistic), with U the utility and with X the operarive subject, we can express the useful act with the formula

$$\frac{t' \, U \, X}{t'' \, X}$$

b) Act of liberality

If the act is designed useful as well as its own behalf and also on behalf of another entity Y, the case can be expressed in the formula

$$\frac{t' \, U \, X}{t'' \, (X + Y)}$$

in which both parties participate in the hedonistic moment of the act in place of X.

c) Contract of corresponding performance

When considering a swap contract between the two entities X and Y, since each acting on its own behalf and others, the act can be expressed in the contract sum of the following elements:

$$\frac{t' \cup X}{t''(X+Y)} + \frac{t' \cup' Y}{t''(X+Y)} + U''$$

Is in fact carried in the contract an additional utility (U") that emerges from the following consideration. If you speculate two acts of reciprocal donation is obtained *ex post* an identical result to that of a swap contract. It is obvious that if the parties instead of establishing two acts of donation establish a mutual agreement, it means that there is a reason for doing the obvious consideration that everyone is willing to give his performance only and when they are getting the counter-performance by the other party. This prediction of the behaviour of others as a condition of it therefore, the conventional element of the contract. This means that in a utility contract resides different and superior to that of the services and of the consideration. That's why the utility of performance and counter-performance - that are credit values - must be added the further conventional utility U" with the participation of both parties. Therefore, the swap contract may be expressed in the formula

$$\frac{t' \cup + U' + U'' (X+Y)}{t'' (X+Y)}$$

where t' and t" are, respectively, the phase of the instrumental and the hedonistic value; U and U' are respectively the values of performance and counter-performance and U" the usefulness of the contract that - as stated above – is in addition to those traded.

d) conventional monetary value. The induced value

In the monetary issuing it is established a convention that produces mere utility without creating exchange.
Being here the convention in order to measure the value of goods and having each unit of measure the quality corresponding to that of the object to be measured, such as the meter has the quality of the length measurement because the length, so the currency has value because it measures the quality of the value.
Thus it was born the monetary value embedded in the symbols of legal tender, without any other cost that the mere activity of mental group (which is precisely the Convention) and its formal manifestation (paper money).

If you then expresses U^m with the conventional monetary value and with A, B, C, D, ... N individuals who accept change, monetary agreement may be expressed in the following formula:

$$\frac{t' \, U^m \, (A + B + C + ... N)}{t'' \, U^m \, (A + B + C + ... N)}$$

....
$t^n \, U^m$ .... etc..

Occurs in this case, the persistence of the value incorporated in monetary symbol U^m because the unit of measurement is in itself a good at repeat-use.
That's why - we repeat - there is a clear distinction between the conventional value of the currency and its own value credit value of the bill. The promissory note is extinguished by the payment, the currency continues to circulate after each transaction indefinitely.
Because this value is independent from inter-relationships required, binds to such an extent in which the symbol is built to look like even a property of matter: the so-called intrinsic value of gold or gold paper. That is that the currency despite being a *legal case* - being an intangible asset recorded value conventional (currently unduly burdened with debt) - is the subject of property rights in all jurisdictions.
We can therefore conclude that the element defined in the formula U^m is an *induced value* that was born in the monetary symbol similarly to what happens in the creation of electricity which arises in the dynamo.
In the dynamo energy source is the magnetic field produced by the electrodes, similarly to what happens in creation of the monetary values caused by a field of conventional relationships, ie by a beam of weather behaviour of others as a condition of, which binds all citizens. Everyone is in fact willing to accept against commodity the currency because expected to give money against goods.
Since the currency is conventional measure of the value, and then the value of the measure (and each unit of measure is conventionally established), in a symbol born the induced value that is the value of the measure that determines the birth of a new good.
As with the dynamo - for induction physical - mechanical energy is transformed into electrical energy, so with the currency - for legal induction - turns the conventional value, a *fumus iuris* (prima facie[A]), in the real value of an asset to be property rights: the currency.[9]

13. The monetary rarity

Once proven that money is the measure of the value of economic goods, which are like that because they are limited in amount, an essential characteristic of the currency is its relative rarity, and this is because each unit must have the quality corresponding to that of the object to be measured.

Traditionally, this problem was solved by using gold as a robe of monetary values. The rarity of gold was, in fact, the natural guarantee of the rarity of the currency. This system, however, had the serious defect of cause economic downturns because the increases of the monetary resources were not adequate to the potential of increases in production.

The criterion of quantitative limitation natural, own gold, now has to be replaced the following criterion objective of technical discretion.

Given that the market price is not only the index of the value of assets, but also the saturation point of the market, when the price tends to coincide with the cost of production must be stopped both the issue monetary and the increase of real goods.

The monetary increases will be so spontaneously commensurate with the size of the population and the needs of increases in production.

These increases in cash must therefore be carried out with a formal procedure consists of three elements:

1) the advertising constitutive
2) the watermark,
3) the recording.

The result of this process will be the birth of the nominal money recorded as an intangible asset, which has, in virtue of induction, the characteristic of being conventional and real, that is subject to property right, namely the currency as a movable good (registered) because it is intended for circulation.

14. Money as a social law instrument. Monetary reform, labour costs.

With the identification of induced values can thus be induced to abolish the tax deductions. In fact, once created the currency for their citizens, rather than distribute it and get it back through tax deductions, it will be possible for the State to create them directly and use it for social purposes in the form of administration of a wealth of collective ownership.

1) Monetary Reform. The induced value of money.

The stumbling block in front of which were found economists, and especially the monetarists, was the inability to explain the nature and cause of the monetary value. In particular, they do not understand why a conventional value - or if you will, a *fumus iuris* (prima facie) - can objectify a real asset in the subject of right of property: the currency.

Traditionally, this value was caused by the fact that, considering the value as a way of being of the currency, are purported to define the monetary value as "intrinsic" to gold. Abolished the gold standard, then, and as a logical consequence of this premise, it is purported to justify the monetary value on the basis of the reserve gold deposited in the bank. Except that even this construction has ceased to exist after the abolition of the Bretton Woods Agreements. Today the currency has the role of the credit, but we all know that it is not. The expression reproduced on banknotes is typical of bearer promissory note signed, only formally, by the Central Bank's Governor (eg. "I promise to pay the bearer on demand the sum of").

That the note is a fake bill emerges from the fact that if the bill is presented for collection, the bank does not pay and is authorized by law to not pay nor with gold, nor with another value.

2) Cost of work - Social Law: established the category of induced values will finally be able to use the money also as an instrument of social law, integrating the rights of the human person through a new law with patrimonial content whose object the money.

It made actually participant every citizen of the property and income of the capital administered by the State and of the creation of money, you can finally free from contractual conflict that the world of work still moves on misunderstandings of Marx's theory of surplus value.

The union, in fact, built with the purpose of claim against the employer as an increase in the surplus

wages, has not made the distribution of income, but rising costs, because the wage is a cost of production. It has caused so an endless spiral of rising prices, rising inflation, further increase in wages, in a permanent conflict. On this basis it is instead to give every citizen a share of monetary income and therefore capital in addition to wages. It is freed in this way, the work report from the illusion to realize an impossible and chimerical social law which, as such, moreover, goes beyond the natural purpose of the enterprise. Once guaranteed to every citizen a minimum of wealth and strengthened the traditional position of the weaker contracting party, the employment contract will have to return to have force in accordance with the principle of "take his word" that returns to the worker his dignity and the employer the certainty of forecasting and planning of production cycles and related costs.

The establishment of a universal social law also frees wages from the burden of social charges.

15. Credit value and monetary value (conventional).

This strategy of market dominance was based on the confusion, therefore, deliberately intended, among two concepts: of credit value and conventional value. While credit value is defined as those relating to the service which is object of loan, for the conventional value, however, it must be considered the value that is caused by the same Convention.

To clarify this difference, it is useful to give an example: if you establish two acts of reciprocal donation between two person, there is *ex post* an identical result to that of a swap contract. And it is evident that if two people, instead of doing two acts of donation, make a contract, it means that there is a specific incentive so that in contract performance corresponding utility resides a different and superior to that of the service and the counter-service. This value is caused by the conventional prediction of the others' behaviour as condition of their own. This is what happens to the currency, the value of which is determined by the simple fact that everyone is willing to give money against goods in anticipation of being able to give itself currency against commodity. The monetary values explode thus, through a pure mental activity of the components of the national communities that realize, with the Monetary Agreement, the value of the currency.

In passing off the form of credit title as conventional value, the banking system achieved the purpose of appropriate the conventional values produced by the community. In fact, it took advantage of the fact that the issuance of debt securities is the prerogative of the debtor, appearing as debtor in the deed statement, and arrogating to itself the right to issue the title, it acquired the ownership of the money. With this system, the bank could turn an apparent debt in a substantial enrichment. For example, the tenor of the note document "*A thousand lire payable to bearer*" would mean that only theoretically, performing this document to the bank, it should be required to pay the equivalent commodity gold. And since, by law, the Bank does not can convert into gold the monetary titles (notes), it is authorized to issue this bill, which is a false a bill of exchange, because it is without expiration term and responsability, and then with the "guarantee" to not pay it.

The bank thus realizes a profit equal to the difference between nominal value and cost of printing currency, turns its debt apparent in a substantial enrichment by means of a macroscopic accounting reversal of which no one is shocked because too obvious, and that allows the banking system to take control of a value that has nothing to do with credit.

While the credit is extinguished by the payment, the money continues to circulate after each transaction indefinitely. And being, moreover, the currency the means to meet and settle the credit, it can not have the same value of credit, even if the credit is sometimes used as a substitute for currency (for example, the bill of exchange used as a means of payment). This is proof that money, even if circulating usually under the guise of credit instrument, incorporates a purely conventional value. The category of Conventional values is still almost completely ignored by economists and by the legal system, so much so that there is still not a valid legal system on the monetary nature. According to traditional theories, when it talks on value, mostly mistakenly refers to the value for costs, such as incorporation of the production cost.

It is historically proven that whenever it is usual to consider a commodity as currency symbol, its value is increased significantly. Because in fact the value of an asset is proportional to its usefulness when a specific goods, in addition to meeting the need for which is naturally destined to be the measure that also satisfies the value for the exchange, obviously increases in value because it increases utility. This happened for example at the beginning the American colonial history in the southern states for tobacco and rice, where the goods were considered as money.

The currency has value for the simple fact that it is the unit of measure of the value of the goods. Each unit has, in fact, the quality corresponding to what must be measured. As the meter has the quality of the length because it measures the length, as the kilogram has the quality of weight because the is the weight measurement, so the currency has the quality of the value because it measures the value. And the value of the currency is conventional, moreover, because each unit is conventionally established.

To be aware of this truth is to discover the enormous potential value of our mental activity of group, so much so that the monetary value exists even when the monetary symbol is zero cost and lacking any form of reserve, as at this day for the dollar and Special Drawing Rights.

That the currency had the dual distinction of being the unit of measure of the value of the goods and then to incorporate the value of the same unit of measurement, it was clearly established by Ezra Pound[10]: "*Money is not an instrument simple as a spade, contains two elements: that of which measures the prices in the market and the one that gives the power to buy the goods.*"

It follows that the monetary function is cause of a duplication of values and doubles at least the wealth of nations that adopt it, because the sum of the units (currency) expresses an amount of value corresponding to that of all the measured or measurable in real assets in the value. It is time that the public becomes realize that those who create the value of money is not who print or issues it, but those who accept it as a means of payment, that is, the community of citizens. The lack of this awareness, causes that who appropriates the monetary value are not the people, but the international banking system, by virtue of the cultural monopoly of the category of conventional values.

16. Relevance of form and legal institutionalization in the creation of monetary value.

It should be specified which technical characteristics take on the process of issuing the creation of monetary value, and in particular the vital importance of the legal institutionalization (so-called legal tender) and the consequent formal manifestation using the currency symbol that cost nothing. It is the formal manifestation of the symbol, once enacted by the community, determines the typical legal significance for social consciousness. It is this that creates the conventional monetary value, so that at the very moment in which it is embedded in the symbol of the value, objectifies in a new good: money.

This good has the qualities of being:

a) intangible
b) collective
c) to have a value conditional.

a) Intangible because the instrumentality lies not in the material of the element symbol (whose function is to show the good, locate it as a matter of right, to attribute it the ownership to the bearer of the document) but in the Monetary Convention. In confirmation of this is the fact that, if you declare a currency not legal tender, it, without lose its physical integrity, it loses its value. This is because the symbol has lost its legal significance. In short, because it has failed the social convention which attributed to the typical symbol of the monetary value.
The legal significance is the typical convention that currently make any useful way of being of legal instruments.
It is worth remembering at this point the masterly definition of Pedius:
"Conventionis nomen generale est omnia pertinens quod faciunt qui inter se agunt"[11].
From these obvious considerations the absolute unreliability of the theories that captiously and interestingly purporting to describe the currency as a commodity, that is as tangible property. These theories are usually incurred to defend the cultural monopoly of monetary science, diverting the mass culture on false tracks of materialist conception of value. The merchandise has always

been the form or outward manifestation of the Monetary value and only within these limits is acceptable its instrumentality or the value if you prefer.

Even gold has value of money not because it is gold, but because there was agreed that it has. So much so that, which is now normally uses the card to perform the function traditionally assumed by gold and nobody offended if you currently use gold-paper, ie currency formally expressed by a symbol of cost null.

When you stand out from the tangible and intangible based on the consideration that the former would be perceived through the senses (*qui tangi possunt*) and the second by means of the intellect, do not understand the essential point of function of the form.

Even the intangibles in fact occur by means of a sensitive medium, eg paper and ink in the copyright or in the design patent or intellectual work.

So this is not the criterion for distinguishing between the two categories of goods. The truth is that material goods are distinguished from intangible assets, because for those the instrumentality resides in matter, in these instead resides in a spiritual reality.

The value that is the element common to all assets - both those materials that those tangibles - always consists of a spiritual reality, that is - as we said - in a forecast, which is a dimension of the spirit because it is a way to be in the time. Just as it is not conceivable the life without time, it is not conceivable value without life, so much so wealth that does not exist in a world of the dead. It is therefore our living experience that makes us aware of this truth. If the currency was purely and simply the goods, ie matter, it would be conceivable even in a world without life. For *reductio ad absurdum*, therefore, this argument must be rejected.

b) collective as it has the characteristic of being at a time the *conventional unit of measurement of the value of goods* and *value of the same measure*, therefore, becomes the object of exchange.

It is the same community that accepting the money as the unit of measure and a means of payment creates and maintains the value, so that the money would not be conceivable only as part of a community that uses it. This characteristic assumes major importance in the international monetary system, because when to this monetary convention participating different States, was born a common interest in stability and defence of monetary values which is a stimulus to the peaceful coexistence and the coordination of economy.

c) to have a *value influenced* by the existence of goods to be measured in the value. This condition is common in any unit of measure. And this is one important qualification to avoid the misunderstanding to believe the currency

"Representative" of the value of the goods on the market as if it were a kind of way of credit or belief of deposit.
The monetary value is, in fact, as we have seen, conventional and non-credit.

Be aware of this truth also means understanding that, at the time of birth, this good must also be adjusted as a matter of jurisprudence; that is it must be established by law, at the time of monetary issuance, to who is the ownership of the currency. A viable reform of the monetary system does not accept the fundamental principle of consider each people owner of its own currency. It is in fact, the community of citizens with its mental activity to create the conventional monetary value.
As we have already said, and we return to remember, the value of money is created by the fact that everyone is willing to accept money against commodity because in turn expects to be able to exchange currency against commodity (NoA Overmore: because the state demanding payment of taxes through this currency). This behaviour prediction of others as a condition of that of himself is the source of monetary value.
So, every people must be recognized as the owner of its currency as it is himself who creates it. Failure of clarification of this concept has allowed the secular misunderstanding on monetary issuance. The bank, in fact, it is given itself the ownership of money because the money was issued by indebtedness of the market, lending it, and since lend money has always been the prerogative of the owner, with a reversal accounting, it was given ownership of the currency, the value of which is, instead, created by citizens. Particularly significant and revealing the consideration of Ezra Pound: "*The great debt that (our friends the) capitalists (of Europe) will see to it is made out of the war must be used to control the volume of money. . . . It will not do to allow the greenback, as it is called, to circulate . . . for we cannot control them*"[12].

17. Brief overview of the historical evolution of monetary symbols that cost nothing.

One can not understand how it was possible the historical realization of the monetary sovereignty, unless you consider the fundamental experience of the Jewish people after the exodus from Egypt. This people stopped and lived for forty years in the wilderness of Sinai, in a historical period when the economy was predominantly agricultural. To survive had no other alternative than to spend the treasure stolen from Egyptian, consuming permanently the acquired wealth, or find an expedient to appropriate, without cost, of goods produced by other peoples.
It is historically proven that the Jewish people, instead of buying the goods by the gold and silver, introduced in market as a means of payment, securities

representing gold and silver, and foreign merchants were well willing to buy these symbols (Mamré or Memra) instead of coins, both because, using the titles representative avoided the risk of being robbed by raiders (not having any culture they did not depicted in the Scriptural symbols any monetary value), and because they had in the symbol of the maximum confidence, since this bill issued by a member of the Israelite nation was solidly guaranteed by all the Jewish community.

We can not explain, in fact, the absolute confidence recognized by the market to the documentary symbol, as if it was itself gold, if you do not consider the powerful influence that the Jewish people had in some fundamental commandments mosaics. Moses commanded his people to the mutual obligation of the loan in case of need and the remission of debts every seven years, in occasion of the so-called Sabbaticcal year (Deuteronomy 15: 1-6). In collective accordance with these precepts, for the Jew was indifferent to lend or not to lend money to his brother, because having lent money, each one of them was in a position to demand the loan from another Jew and was also uninteresting that in the sabbatical you had a remission of debts because - no matter how great it was the amount of debt paid off - it was always in the position of being able to restart it at the beginning of the new seven years.

From these Mosaics commandments derived that every time the bill was presented for encashment, it was regularly paid, because the insolvent debtor could apply for a loan to another Jew, and him granted it because the religious commandment, as such as because, if in turn he had need of money, he could claim it against another member of the Jewish people. So it happened that every credit instrument issued by any component of the Israelite people, was supported by the joint liability of all the Jews.

The certainty of fulfilment became such that, who was holding the title of credit, felt more comfortable hold it with him, rather than presenting it to the collection. In fact, the value originally planned as achievable to expiry of the loan, ie the presentation to the collection, it became a value obtained immediately by possession of the document, for legal certainty and the confidence born from mercantile experience. It was in fact the legal certainty to cause in the *Animus* of the creditor bearer of the title, the anticipation at the present moment of the expected values as achieveble at the time of maturity and to ensure that the title of credit had immediately a new value, current and autonomous. So we can explain how the bearer is considered satisfied of credit represented in the title (Memré), without presenting it to the collection, by the mere fact of holding the document.

It was modified in this way, the original nature of the document because this was losing out the credit nature to take that of conventional monetary value. That is why in practice the mercantile document issued by the Monetary member of the Jewish people acquired a value equal to or even greater than that of gold.

The monetization of debt as a way to peddle currency that cost nothing is acutely sensed by Ezra Pound when he says: "*The Bank of England was based on the discovery that, instead to lent money, you would able to lent the bills (promissory note) of the Bank*".[13]

It is clear that, on this basis, has originated a real strategy of domination in which the banking system is able to get into debt the markets of monetary value that creates out of nothing, and with much greater efficiency, since the incorporation of the value of money in the paper symbols, corresponds to the simultaneous demonetization of gold, silver and in general of all the coins-traditional goods.

It is obvious that, with the issuance and circulation of gold paper, much of the purchasing power of money was extracted from commodity symbols and built-in symbols that cost nothing. This alteration of the monetary equilibrium was also one of the determinants of political systems. Thus, for example, is not without significance to the fact that the decay of the Roman Empire it occurs simultaneously with the clipping of the coins, made by emperors to fill the monetary gaps caused in the taxation by the demonetization of gold. So you were forced to maintain an adequate monetary liquidity, to reduce the weight of the coins minted or merge precious metals in base metals, as is proved by numismatic history.[14]

The banking system has, therefore, understood that, by moving the Monetary Convention from goods to the symbol that has zero cost, of which, moreover, controlled the monopoly to issue by the privilege legislatively recognized, could achieve the result to appropriate the monetary value created by the market. On this principle, through subsequent gradual steps, the banking system has extracted from gold most, if not even, in some cases, the totality of the value of gold.

The demonetization of gold, resulting in this strategy of market dominance, has taken away at the traditional economic and political head, the monetary value at their disposal, that is, their own economic potential, and with it, the political sovereignty. It is thus achieved a form macroscopic and occult-profit organization, where the coffers full in gold of the monarchies of old Europe and all savers, which were traditionally accustomed to do rely on this symbol money were not emptied of their content material, but the content immaterial value. On these assumptions, the decay of political systems is regularly caused by the explosion of debts which, not surprisingly, in history has always coincided with the demonetization of gold. Once extracted from gold its monetary value, it was purchased by the banking system, that is, from the producers of monetary symbols with cost null, which became the new masters of the world.

The realization of this tool was made possible by the absolute rule of the form (monopoly issue), as well as cultural awareness that the incorporation of the conventional value in the symbol allows the ability to objectify the value in a new good, manifest, held it and assign the ownership to the bearer of the document. On this premise, since the first bearer is the issuer, the bank is credited with the ownership of money that emits, so much so that issues and lending it, as you know, lent money is an exclusive prerogative of the owner. The famous phrase from William Paterson, founder of the Bank of England: *"The bank hath benefit of interest on all moneys which it creates out of nothing"*, which appears unscrupulously honest, in effects hides the most important part of the truth, because it is not true that the dealer is enriched only by interest, but also and above all of the same currency, the value of which - as we have seen - is not created by the bank, but by the collectivity.

Upon of monetary issuance it has been applied the principle of a well-known schools of high diplomacy, for which, when you want to accept a condition that the counterparty would never have accepted if he had were aware, you put that clause as implicit part of the contract. So it is that those who take money loan from a bank of issue explicitly acknowledges himself as debtor, but implicitly makes two other statements far more important, that he does not realize, because he recognizes to the documents received the quality of money and at the same time it gives the ownership to the bank, because to lend money is a prerogative of owner.

For nationality of a currency shall not be construed therefore that the community of that nation is the owner of that currency, but, conversely, that they have been expropriated and indebted on the issue by the central bank of that nation. It is as if some persons ask to its own cashier, and instead of just saying "give me money" tell him "lend me money". In that moment he realizes a macroscopic reversal accounting for where the money is no longer his own, but of the cashier. Exactly in these terms it is the relationship that is established between the government or the community of that country and the their central banks.

It is obvious that this serious degeneration of the monetary system can be eliminated only in rectifying at the source the basic defect.

The ownership of the money on the issue must be subtracted to the system of central banks and returned to the national communities, which means to replace the "bank notes" whit "state notes", similarly to what happened with American *greenbacks*, before the Civil War.

18. Characteristics of monetary form and its implications on monetary

regimes.

Once shown that the currency symbol is nothing else that the manifestation of a formal legal case, it is necessary to highlight some essential characteristics of this "*phenomenon*". It should first be noted that the formal manifestation differs from the natural manifestation because, while this coincides with the phenomenon and it subsist contextually with it, the formal manifestation does not always coincide with the creative moment of the submitted legal case.

You may have in fact the concurrency between form and legal content, when the normative will is manifested by conclusive behaviour, eg. the implicit contract. When the formal manifestation is instead consolidates into a creative process of the symbol, this can not be contextual to its content. Usually it is that the parties, before they want a particular legal relationship, and then manifest it. It consider the case of composition of negotiation acts that is completed after the parties have agreed the object. Here you have a chronological sequence between the acceptance of the contract and its formal manifestation. For the most the juridical experience put us in front of the cases in which the formal event is consecutive to the activity volitional creator of the rule.

In the monetary manifestation it occurs, instead, a reverse of chronological order between the creative moment of the legal case and the creative moment of its formal manifestation (monetary symbol). In fact it occurs in practice that the central bank, by printing monetary symbols, prepares the legal form which has then its content of conventional value at the time when the first borrower, accepting as money the symbol, he gives the corresponding value. Who in fact cause the value of money is not who print or issue, but who accepts it as a means of payment, that is, the community of citizens. *The first borrower of money, under the thumb of conditioned reflex to consider the formal manifestation successive to the creation of its legal content, has considered the currency already existing as asset in the hands of the body of issue, while they had nothing else that the mere symbols still empty of their monetary value.*

This is explained as well as initial equivocation, that you have not connected the money to the genus of the legal case, both derived a macroscopic reversal of legal and accounting truth at the time of issue the money.

The first borrower of money, not realizing that it was himself, as a member of the community, to create the conventional monetary value by the mere fact of accepting the money, was induced to accept it, not free as would have been right, but with the counter-part of debt.

"It is happened in this way that central banks have expropriated and indebted the national communities because they have issued by lending money, and

lend money is a prerogative of the owner. In other words, the first the borrower of money has considered the monetary value as existing in the hands of those who controlled the production of symbols, setting the stage for a paradoxical parasitism operated by central banks to the detriment of national communities. The currency came into existence as an intangible asset so burdened with debt, so that the legal nature of
this symbol is to build up debt and precarious ownership of money for the bearer, such as precarious is the ownership of the debtor, because he has it until such time as the returns to the creditor. The real *dominus* (dominant) is only the creditor: the bank.
This situation was mitigated by the nature of things when the symbol was commodity money (gold), because, existing gold in the market, was consolidating in the hands of the bearer of the goods a potential value of a horizontal vision of monetary sovereignty of which also participated the market. When money became the symbol at no cost, it exploded in a vertical structure, an absolute and unlimited hegemony of monetary issuing bodies.

Never before, then, there is the need to prepare a legal regulation on monetary values, after has define the nature, causes and characteristics, as we have said, of an intangible asset as legal case. It should first be noted that the ownership of the money must be declared at the time of issuance, exclusively attributable to the national community, because it is only on this premise that you will be able to determine who should be the owner, who is the creditor or the debtor and it will finally can determine to who should be given that potential value in which consolidates the monetary sovereignty. In the formalization of the symbol the expression of monetary value should not be signed by the Governor of the central bank, as at this day, but by the President of State, which is the only one who can legitimately represent the collective ownership of the currency.

It will then competence of economists to propose on criteria of rigid technical discretion, the amount of currency to be issued in order to comply with the stability of the monetary value, indispensable quality of every unit, but shall, instead, be the exclusive competence of political sovereignty and the legislative function determine of who should be the ownership of the money, and who the creditor and who the debtor. This in order to purify the monetary systems from those fundamentals misunderstandings that have until now allowed some unacceptable forms of arbitrary depletion and parasitism, to the detriment of national communities.

For this, there is the need to establish within the rule of law a "*Department of the currency*" – in replacement of the central bank - to allow clear transparency with the production and distribution of money among all members of the national community.

Notes to Chapter II:

[A] Prima facie: and is a Latin expression meaning on its first encounter or *at first sight*. The literal translation would be "at first face" or "at first appearance", from the feminine form of *primus* ("first") and *facies* ("face"), both in the ablative case. In modern, colloquial and conversational English, a common translation would be, "on the face of it". The term ***prima facie*** is used in modern legal English (including both Civil Law and Criminal Law) to signify that upon initial examination, sufficient corroborating evidence appears to exist to support a case. In common Law jurisdictions, *prima facie* denotes evidence that, unless rebutted, would be sufficient to prove a particular proposition or fact. The term is used similarly in academic philosophy. Most legal proceedings, in most jurisdictions, require a *prima facie* case to exist, following which proceedings may then commence to test it, and create a ruling. ((https://en.wikipedia.org/wiki/Prima_facie)

Fumus boni iuris: is a Latin phrase, used in European courts, meaning "likelihood of success on the merit of the case" (literal meaning: "smoke of a good right"), being a requirement for admission to certain benefits (for example, legal aid) or pronunciation of certain court actions (for example, so-called protective measures, injunctions). It has a ***prima facie*** case when there is a possibility that the right claimed exists in practice: the existence of this assumption should be examined by the court which will decide according to the results of the fait accompli.
(https://en.wikipedia.org/wiki/Fumus_boni_iuris)

[9] See above "The University D'Annunzio" - Magazine information of the University, from January to August 1992 "The induced value of money", p. 29-31.

[10] Ezra Pound, Lavoro e usura. All'insegna del paese d'oro. Scheiwiller, Milan, 1972, p. 19.
[11] Digesto 2, 14: 1, 3.
[12] Ezra Pound, a. quote., p. 69.
[13] Ezra Pound, a. quote, p. 69.
[14] We can not avoid in this regard, from refuting the argument put forward by authoritative doctrine in which the decadence of the Roman Empire is to be attributed to the advent of Christianity, which as bearer instead of values of

natural law could harmonize with the Roman tradition.

Chapter III

Principles and guidelines for a reform of the monetary system

19. The futility of the monetary reserve.

From these premises, we can finally clear up the traditional misunderstanding to derive the value of money by the goods placed in its warranty (reserve). If this was true, the dollar not covered by gold and not convertible into gold, after explicit statements of Nixon in August 1971, should not have any value, as well as the same **Special Drawing Rights** issued by the International Monetary Fund as a reserve currency. You could still grant a semblance of confidence to the advocates of the need of the monetary reserve (to give purchasing power to a currency conceived as a title of credit), until were in force the Bretton Woods Agreements.
But today, after the repeal of this Convention, to maintain the dollar as a reserve currency, it means
explicitly agree to a real colonial subordination on the U.S. banking system.
In fact, while the dollar - without gold reserves - has the international recognition of legitimate currency, it does not happens for other currencies, bound to the need for a reserve in dollars. As if to say that while the dollar, without reserve, has the value of gold, it does not happen to other currencies.
The broad lines of monetary policy world today are based on the theory of double truth. While for banks which issuing a reserve currency is the principle by which the monetary value is purely conventional, for the other issuing banks (and even more so for those that do not issue money), it is worth the principle that the currency has a credit value as conceived as a pseudo-faith deposit reserve of currency (the credit). We can say that the international banking system is governed by a hierarchical structure of feudal type, in which, by imperial sovereignty of the banks that issue reserve currency depends, for spontaneous germination, a proliferation of colonial banks. For economy of expression and for conceptual accuracy, we propose to define as imperial banks those capable of making a reserve currency and other *colonial banks* (commercial banks), those to issue their own currency (credit), need, or rather, have the need to establish a *reserve* currency.
Given that money is the measure of the value of economic goods, because these are limited in the amount and that each measurement units must have the quality corresponding to that of the object to be measured, even the currency must necessarily be "rare."
When the money was gold, the rarity of gold was the natural assurance of the monetary rarity on the following principle:
Given that the price is not the only index of the value of goods, but also the

point of saturation of the market – for we say that the market is saturated when the price tends to coincide with the cost of production - when this trend occurs, the market is saturated with both goods and money. In this case we agree to suspend contextually both the production of new goods, that the issuance of new money.

20. The rarity money as a tool of domination.

It is obvious that the current structure holds the cultural monopoly of the top banks. Only on this basis, the large public deculturalized is addicted to assess, as a natural phenomenon, that the currency is sometimes maddeningly rare.

""*To say that a state cannot pursue its aims because there is no money* - says an anonymous remembered by Ezra *Pound - is like saying that an engineer cannot build roads because there are no kilometres"*.[15]

The rarity of the currency symbol, traditionally caused by the rarity of the goods with which the symbol was coined (gold), today is accepted as a fact completely normal, despite being the reserve currency producible without limit and without cost, in quantities arbitrarily established by the leaders of the imperial banks. At the present state of things, all the peoples of the world are reduced to the level of colonies of the international banking system, with the aggravating circumstance of not know, because all monetary policy initiatives are promoted on the assumption that the reserve is necessary to give to the respective national currencies its value.

With this system the imperial banks take from the colonial banks every discretion, any freedom of decision, to adapt the monetary gains to the economic development of their country. When, in fact, these increases are commensurate with the amount of money as reserve, are basically established by the imperial banks. The currency it is like the blood: its quantity must be proportionate to the size of the body being treated.

To realize this truth is enough to consider an elementary example: if there are ten pens on the market and ten dollars, you can sell the pens at an average unit price of a penny, but if you have to produce ten other pens, you will have to put on the market ten more dollars, lest it be able to sell the pens at a price of sixpence. And if the pen cost for example sixty cents, it is obvious that the production process, in the absence of increase in monetary liquidity, it stops.

This means that every freedom to make decisions on the development or the economic downturn of the markets, it is not in the hands producers of real goods, but in those of the banking system[16] which produces a reserve currency.

21. Recent developments in international monetary policy.

This has been proven by recent events in the U.S. monetary policy. To determine a serious situation of hardship and economic recession of global dimensions was enough for the American monetary authorities to program an increase in interest on bank deposits, so that economic operators had greater convenience to keep money in the bank rather than investing in productive activities. In this way to the damage of the vacuum money, cause of severe economic recession in all markets operating in the dollar area, it has added the further disadvantage of distorting the very function of money, used as purely speculative to make money with other money (high bank interest rates), rather than the his own function to promote productive work of goods and services.

This was made possible with the U.S. monetary authorities, without any risk, because having them the hegemonic control of the reserve currency, were and are in condition to produce money without other costs that typographic symbols of money and no limit other than determined by its sole will. There is explains how the cash flows are characterized by an alternation of abundance or monetary rarity, on which speculates the occult society that use instrumentalization of the system.

The countries that are indebted with the American Central Bank (the Federal Reserve Bank) to get availability of reserve currency, have seen their debt increase heavily. It is obvious the fact that with the appreciation of monetary base (made rare with the artful policy of high interest rates) of over 100%, increase in equal value of debts and credits, to the benefit of the creditor and damage of debtor[17].

In this circumstance the international monetary system has expressed its serious flaws, obvious signs of its defect at the origin to have conceived the international monetary system on the prejudice of the need for reserves, in addition for a national currency (dollar standard).

The monetary function of our time is a straight reversal of the macroscopic objectives that should normally characterize the functional competence of the banking bodies.

While the normal organic is governed by the obvious principle that the organ (of a body) is at the service of the community, but here, the national communities are parasitically exploited by the monetary bodies, so that we might well say that, when Bank of America lends dollars, or when the International Monetary Fund lends **Special Drawing Rights** to allow issuing banks (commercial banks of credit) the availability of reserve money, they are not these banking organizations to serve national communities, but vice versa these communities are parasitically exploited, as they are to borrow unnecessarily for a value (the reserve currency) equal to that of their money. This is done with the belief in the necessity of having to do it and have to be grateful for the granting of the loan, in the regards of those who granted it.

One can therefore say that the whole international monetary system is deformed by a defect at the origin that we define, according to the Spencerian formula, as a real "prejudice teleological". H. Spencer, the well-known English sociologist, defined for that fact *"for which an act is considered necessary or not, depending not on the its actual practical utility, but as is consistent or not to the established cult."*

In short, the need of the monetary reserve has origin from the simple belief that the reserve is required. It is this a way of being of the instrumentalization for the purposes of power of the Hegelian idealism, for which, having reduced the reality at the idea of reality, it has reduced the state of necessity at the idea of necessity.

The Hegelian philosophy allows, in the field of the moral sciences, an arbitrary construction of the truth. In fact, when it reduces reality to the idea of reality[18], it conceives the same thought as capable of imagining the reality itself, ie to build any form of truth as long as feasible. True thus becomes everything and the opposite of everything.

On this belief it has created the only colonial empire of our time, in which the functional organization hierarchical not straight on the principle of service for the community, but on the discrimination of a privileged top power which defends its hegemony over the cultural monopoly in the category of conventional values.

This empire is so much more efficient than the political, that it was decided to abolish the old colonies based on subjection to let them stay in such a subordination far more drastic: than the debt.

22. Organic society and instrumental subjectivity. The SO-CALLED inverted pyramid

We have built on these premises in the structure of society, a form of so-called inverted pyramid.

This term, which appeared recently in the parliamentary proceedings[19], deserves to be regarded particularly because it can occur the full awareness of its meaning. It is obvious that one can not speak of inverted pyramid if you do not have the preliminary definition of the straight pyramid.

Sociologists normally intend for that the so-called organic society, in which the organ is acting in the name and on behalf of itself and others. The best expression of this type of social structure is the well-known fable of Menenius Agrippa in speech to the common people of Rome. With the aphorism of the limbs rebelled to the stomach with damage throughout the body, it stresses the fact that the body produces the usefulness of its typical functional activity, equally enjoyed by all limbs.

If you indicate with a point the unit-organ that produces the functional utility and with a series of points, ie with a flat, the community that enjoys the organic function, the union of the vertex point with the basic flat, it emerges the structure of the straight pyramid.

On this premise the concept of society come from the circular connection of the following definitions. Given that:

a) the *organ* consists of individuals who exercise the function;
b) the *function* is the activity put in existence by the organ to serve society members;
c) the *organic relationship* is that one where the organ is acting in the name and on their own and that of others, the society will consist of the individuals linked by the organic relationship. So may be said, in a logical equation, eg. that the commercial contract is up to the buyer and seller bound by the contract, as is the organic relationship to society.

The concept of society in such a case has human content and fulfilled in all the members and the organ, ie in the appearance sociological and historical operating in the organic relationship: *Senatus Populusque Romanus*.

It is this the definition of society according to the Roman and Christian traditions. *Societas sunt homines sunt ibi* here is the realistic and vivid expression of the school glossators. Opposed to this definition is now the society stand on the concept of "inverted pyramid" that has its foundation and logical assumption in the society-subjectivity instrumental expressed with the most varied definitions: personification of the assets, personification of the rule, centre abstract for juridical accusation in the *Fictio Juris* relations, legal person, etc..

All these definitions reduce the society to a concept without human content, and, in our opinion, constitute the symptoms of a serious deformation of value judgements, which ill also the contemporary legal science.

We dare to say that the doctrine, which concerns the company law, has considered all aspects of subjectivity instrumental, except the most important. Since, in fact, it is not conceivable a tool without its use, the society-instrumental presumes an another society with human content: the exploiting society. The fact that theorists of corporate law have ignored this essential aspect of the problem, has meant that it is reduced most of the time the corporate phenomenon to a mere legal formalism.

On this basis, it is explained how certain phenomena are manifested in the context and how, not for case, it happened some real historical coincidences: constitutional state and Freemasonry, ruling class and socialist state, anonymous corporation or multinational and the union's majority shareholder, political party and party trends etc..

This is because Freemasonry is now the society exploiting (which take advantage of) the constitutional state, the ruling class is now the society exploiting the socialist state, the union's majority shareholder is now the society exploiting now the anonymous corporation or multinational, the trend is now the society exploiting the political party.

To correct terminology and concepts we like to clarify that for instrumental subjectivity must be understood that hierarchical order that places as first the instrument and as second place the human person. Because the law is an instrument as it is the result of a creative activity of the spirit, ie the subjectivity instrumental that is the personification of the instrument, it occurs every time that the society is run on the primary instrument and in the personification of the rule: the Social Statute. Once placed the distinction between society-exploiting and society-instrumental, it follows that of the exploited society, which is the community of members. And the ownership, which is apparently of the instrumental societies, it becomes substantially exploiting because these have all the powers that is the right of ownership. It is this, then, the strategy with which minorities culturally more aggressive strip off and dominate the majority.

This is done in the socialist state, in which state property is basically property of the rulers; in the constitutional state, where the domain of the State is that of the Masonic lodges; in the anonymous corporation in which the complex of powers constituting the right to ownership is the union of the majority of shareholders.

The most dangerous aspect of this social pathology lies in the fact that it is a subversion of ethics of the society. (Benedetto Croce said exactly that ethical concerns at the moment of the purpose, the economy than of the means).

While in organic conception of society, ethics is to protect the interests of all members (because here the society consists in the collectivity of members), in the society-instrumental subjectivity, which is a kind of the *legal ghost*, ethics normally consists in the protection of the society-exploiting (which is always a minority) peddled under the guise of protecting the public interest.

This serious deformation rational and ethics is in our opinion the main causes of the decline of our time because all the value judgements involved in social relations resulting deformed and even distorted.

Failure clarification of the premises has determined, in fact, the phenomenon of severe to live on the view of the history the consequences of errors on the level of thought born from a specious and arbitrary legal-philosophical rationalism irreversibly tainted of irrationality.

The science of law must become aware of the fact that you can not enjoy the goods for representation.

It can be attorney in a deal or in a legal act, or in the management of the property, not in the "*quality*" of owner, because the hedonistic moment is a fact connected exclusively to the human person.

The misunderstanding of subjectivity instrumental, built traditionally in monetary sovereignty, today has been extended to other social structures in a real epidemic form of cultural malady.

When in applying the principles of immanence it reduces the reality of the "*I (self) thinking*", that is the reality to the idea of reality, it follows a severe deformation of value judgements because they are crushed into a single entity the time instrumental, which concerns the object, and the hedonistic moment, or purposive, pertains to the subject, exactly because it confused the object with the subject.

To say "personified instrument" or "instrumental subjectivity" is like saying that an instrument may be able to enjoy a good. Thus it happened that the ownership, which is legally protected enjoyment of the goods, was subtracted to the human person and attributed to the personified instrument, that is to say, in fact, to the societies-exploiting the instrumental subjectivities.

With this cultural strategy the society-exploiting have seized the will and voice of the people.

On these misunderstandings have been made possible those judgements of conviction of historic proportions, which was often the sparkle and ferment of the great world wars.

We are convinced that a cultural choice is only valid if the conclusions coincide with common sense.

It deserves to govern a people only who loves him, because only those who loves are willing to serve. The misery of philosophical-legal rationalism, typical of societies-exploiting, it's all here. Only someone who does not love is willing to use instead to serve.

The simple and clear formula of the organic society can, in fact, operate when the organ is at the service of society understood as a community of members[20]. The instrumentality is never primary time of the spirit. The primary time is always the choice of the purpose, to which in a moment logically and chronologically following is commensurate with, and

functionally structured the instrument. We can therefore say that in the hierarchical order in the first place is the man and then the instrument. In the society-subjectivity instrumental, with the reversal of the hierarchical order between regulatory instrument and human person there is an inversion between the mean and the purpose, and then the overthrow of the social pyramid, because those who produce the utility is the community, those who enjoy it is the organ.

In conclusion we can say that the personification of the instrument necessarily correspond to the instrumentalization of the human person. Placed in fact the natural alternation between the finalist moment and instrumental moment in the formulation of value judgements, once it violated the hierarchical order at the origin and denied at the human person the priority that it deserves, it follows a distorted structure of the practical behaviour and of the same organization of social groups.

The individual loses his own ability to be "legal entity" as incapable of enjoying the utility of legal instruments. That's why we can say that social structures laid on the principle of so-called "*Subjectivity instrumental*" or "*personification of the instrument*" are inherently evil.

The greatest manifestation of this organic degeneration, functional and social, it has historically realized in the monetary sovereignty. Who actually produces the monetary value are the citizens, those who appropriate it is the bank and for the bank the not apparent society that exploits it.

Not by chance that all the banking facilities worldwide and the International Monetary Fund are the anonymous corporation, that is, instrumental subjectivity. In all these structures is all too obvious that the substantial power - as shown above - is not in the hands of the summit formally apparent, but not apparent of those society-exploiting.

Only on this basis we can understand the exact scope of the letter sent by one of the Rothschilds to the Kleimer Morton and Vandergould Company of New York on June 26, 1863, remembered by Ezra Pound[21]:

"*..The few who understand the system will either be so interested in its profits or so dependent on its favours that there will be no opposition from that class, while on the other hand, the great body of the people mentally incapable of comprehending the tremendous advantage that capital derives from the system will bear its burdens without complaint and perhaps without even suspecting that the system is inimical to their interests*".

23. The uniform tax law as an instrument of the international monetary system.

On this basis it explained how today has established a uniform tax law as a regulatory instrument at the service of monetary sovereignty and the banking system with serious prejudice to the interests of the national community.

Thus, for example, the value-added tax (VAT) realises a withdrawal of money without consideration[22], right in the moment when it would instead justified an increase of monetary emission[23].

As it is known, in fact, the withdraw here is happen in the moment in which the product is placed on the market, so that occurs together with the increase in real goods and monetary liquidity squeeze.

In this way, the entire tax system is distorted and deformed. While the traditional tribute was the consideration for the functions and services provided by the State, now the purpose of taxation has become the drain up of the monetary market without other consideration than that of "drain it," the pretext of fighting inflationary pressures.

So any increase in production accelerates the simultaneous withdrawal of money, creating a dynamic deflationary that predisposes to failure the manufacturers of real goods and that makes it more prosperous the usury.

The power groups who exploit the banking system can take control of monetary values existing on the market without deprive citizens the ownership of money. To them it is sufficient that the money is subtracted temporarily out of circulation in annual cycles that are renewed annually - just as happens with VAT - for the simple fact that:

a) the remaining money left on the market automatically increases in value, that is, purchasing power exactly proportional to the arbitrary scarcity of money due from the tax;

b) the banking system is always in a position to replace at the printing cost as much currency in place of that taken, thereby achieving not only an enrichment equivalent to that of money removed from circulation, but also the additional profit of the related bank interest.

The money collected from this tax, as it is already in the pockets of economic operator, it is also what he could use without paying bank interest, those which instead will have to pay when he needs money.

The true purpose of Tax Added Value is therefore to allow the banking system to lend to traders their money with usury after have it first withdraw for free.

To realize the seriousness of the drawbacks of the current system is sufficient to consider the enormity of the powers permitted to groups who exploit the system of central banks. While the issue of money is made from the banking system with no other cost than that of the symbol, the payment made by the taxpayer has a real cost, because that money was earned by him as consideration for employment. That is why, having that money substantial value corresponding to the one he legitimately produced, when the revenue picks it up without consideration creates an undue depletion of the taxpayer.

As if that were not enough, the societies-exploiting, the various political and banking systems, having the power to know exactly, because the declaration made by the taxpayer in the usual forms, profit margins, costs and investments, they are also able to dose the amount of the tax, in order to obtain the maximum profit and establish arbitrarily how much to leave to the economic operator as profit margin. To this is added the severe drawback of the induced costs of this tax system to which, falling on the taxpayer the responsibility of the accounting records, that sterilizes a large amounts of working hours, intended as mere accounting activity. And if you think that the tax of added value not only varies from product to product, but also among the various markets, the system is able to cause arbitrary in its sole development or economic recession and where when it wants to, because it is able to alter the profit margins allowed.

It is all too evident that these very serious drawbacks of the system can be eliminated only as long as the tax deductions are made for the sole purpose of covering the costs of the functions and services provided by the state to the community.

24. The heavy money as an instrument of monetary policy.

If you want to eliminate the drawbacks of an excessively devalued currency is not necessary to use the instrument of tax, it is sufficient to adopt the procedure of "weigh down" the money[24] that allows you to increase the value of symbols while leaving unaltered the purchasing power of the monetary aggregates on the market.

To claim to use, as it is this day, the tributary medium to defend the currency from inflationary pressures, means allow the pursuit of unjust privileges causing - as it stated above - the unjust enrichment of the banking system and the undue depletion of the citizens.

Once it shown that the structure of the currency consists of two elements: the material of the symbol and the one intangible of value, we realize that when one attempts to make withdrawals by tax to combat inflation, with the pretext to withdraw money to make it more rare, it is also taken its purchasing power. Under the pretext of so withdraw the formal envelope of the symbol, it also picks up its contents. As if to say that under the pretext of removing the dress it also robs the skin.

In this way not realized a simple expropriation of money (as happens with the tax) but a real confiscation with contents unfairly punitive.

That is why, to allow control of monetary liquidity without prejudice to the vital interests of the market, we need to be conducted at the same time - even with uniform rules of law - the removal of harmful and unjust tax structures such as VAT and the "weigh down" on the currencies.

Once returned to the state monetary sovereignty now usurped by a system of joint-stock companies which are precisely all the banks in the world, it will be possible to abolish the tax law, having the State the ability to control the circulation of money and to meet all the needs of the community with the only two means, the issue of money and "weigh down" of currencies, so that the means would be used for marginal tax forms intervention and always with a view to covering the costs of the functions and services provided by the state.

25. Lines for a reform of the monetary system

The nations could be restored, in our opinion, a substantial monetary sovereignty, and with it political and economic freedom, with the following conditions:

a) that each nation creates its own currency without monetary reserves;
b) that is distinct the moment of creation of the money from that of the distribution;
c) that at the act of creation every people is recognized as the owner of its currency. Once it established in fact that the value of money is conventional, this value should be attributed to those who are participating in the convention, and helps to create it, that is, the community of citizens;
d) that the power to create money is removed from the banking system and returned to the political power, replacing the "*Banknotes*" with "*Statenotes*";
e) that the increases in the monetary issuance is commensurate with the potential for economic development;
f) that the amounts of newly issued, necessary for the purposes of public utility, which today are charged to the State, are instead credited to it and assumed in the availability of government;
g) that tax deductions are made and justified exclusively as consideration of the functions and services rendered by the State to the community;
h) that to control inflation is adopted instead of the heavier tax the procedure of "weigh down" of money;
i) that the currencies are each other freely convertible;
l) that the amounts of newly issued, necessary for productive activities, are lent to economic operators without interest, and once returned after the completion of production cycles, are distributed among the citizens, establishing a new claim with financial content to supplement those of the human person and relevant to the status of citizen.

This will also prepare the distribution of monetary liquidity across the market, so as to eliminate the
drawbacks traditionally defined as overproduction and improperly whereas they were only phenomena underconsumption. In fact, when the distribution of the currency is not widespread among all citizens, it is passes for overproduction not that one in which the production of goods is more than proportionate to the needs, but only the one in which a part of the product (overproduction improper) remains unsold because some Social Class do not have enough monetary liquidity to buy what, however, are they need. This system also ensures the producers themselves for the launch of the new product on the market, for the obvious reason that the sale at fair price of new products is influenced by the issuance of new currency. It can then be applied the elimination of that form of bankruptcy where the companies are forced to

unbalanced budget not for the uneconomic or irrationality of the initiative, but due to unjustified and arbitrary monetary rarity. Under this aspect it must be pointed out that the danger of deflation - in which the increase of goods produced is more than proportional to the of monetary liquidity - is an equally serious problem and in some ways more serious than that of inflation (ndt: in the current system), because it is due to the shut-down of production processes (economic).

These principles will become active as long as the markets are structured so as to realize an organicity such as to make them complete, at least in the availability of basic raw materials.

We realize that each of these arguments implies the need for a thorough analysis, but given the characteristic eminently synthetic of this investigation, we limit ourselves to laying down the basic principles for now.

In short, once again proved that money - even if sometimes take the form of credit instrument - has the value eminently conventional, to achieve a fair international monetary system, it will be necessary to establish a international agreement that embraces:

1) into domestic law of each State the uniform principle of law that people has to be declared owner of the "Own" money on the issue, without reserve, replacing the "bank notes" the "State notes";

2) in international relations the principle of reciprocity in recognition of the value of the currency of others as condition for the recognition of their own, allowing the free convertibility in accordance with the exchange rate regimes. Given the nature eminently conventional of the principle of reciprocity, this is fully capable of causing – for what said above - monetary values in international transactions;

3) gold as a monetary instrument supplementary and subsidiary system with nominal money.

Only in the absence of mutual trust gold can be international currency to pay off balances of countries creditors. The function of gold relative to the nominal money would be subsidiary and limited to cases where there is impossibility of reciprocity in the recognition of other people's money as a condition of recognition of their own.

As established in fact that the principle of reciprocity is valid only between the contracting parties when there is reasonable confidence on the stability of the currency of others, when that trust is lacking, and only in this case, you should consider gold as a monetary instrument used to meet the balances of the countries creditor. In this way, while recognizing to gold its function as currency, the would be allowed to limited function in marginal cases.

On this basis, being interest of all States to use monetary symbols that cost nothing rather than the gold-commodity, it will also be of general interest to limit the function of gold to a minimum, eliminating the positions and drastic alternatives between gold and paper money system.

Before concluding, we would like to emphasize that all of these special purpose functions are unified, as well as an organic technique by the same rational choice and Christian ethics, as opposed to the traditional one, characterizing monetary sovereignty for thousands of years. From these principles it will be possible, in our view, translate into a valid legal system, the instrument to meet the basic need felt by all peoples of the world for a substantial and definitive monetary justice.

We have no illusions that this need can be met with ease: and this not so much because the forces which are opposed, are the largest in the world, but because the major obstacle to a rational system reform is ignorance.

Notes Chapter III:

[15] E.Pound, "What good is the money?", Ed. San Giorgio, Naples, 1980 p.15.

[16] In this sense, the significant step of Brux Adams, (The New Empire, 1903 MacMillan, New York): "*Perhaps no financier has ever lived abler than Samuel Loyd. Certainly he understood as few men, even of later generations, have understood, the mighty engine of the single standard. He comprehended that, with expanding trade, an inelastic currency must rise in value; he saw that, with sufficient resources at command, his class might be able to establish such a rise, almost at pleasure; certainly that they could manipulate it when it came, by taking advantage of foreign exchange. He perceived moreover that, once established, a contraction of the currency might be forced to an extreme, and that when money rose beyond price, as in 1825, debtors would have to surrender their property on such terms as creditors might dictate. "Nihil novi sub sole". It is what is happening today with the overvaluation of the dollar. The banking system has not only the possibility to realize colonial subordination but even to expropriate the the world.*"

[17] It deserves some consideration an important choice of monetary policy, which goes under the name of "heavy money". The heavier of the currency is to replace to the currency in circulation new monetary symbols with a multiple value of the symbols replaced. In this way the new monetary unit has a higher value because the numerical expression of the new symbols has a

smaller amount than that of the replaced symbols (so, eg., the French currency). At first glance this seems completely irrelevant to produce concrete effects in the dynamic of the market since, these, retain the same values, even expressed with monetary units of measurement of different entities. This reasoning, however, does not hold up when one considers that the heavy currency is prepared for a policy of inflation while the light currency is actually designed for a monetary choice deflationary. Which means that a light money serves the interests of the banking system which, being "Owner" of the currency on the issue, tends to increase the purchasing power, whereas the heavy currency is adequate to protect the interests of the producers of real goods because they are interested in a monetary policy to increase liquidity. Usually the monetary authorities to establish a heavy currency
mask a deflationary monetary policy, that is, they operate a simultaneous withdrawal from the market in monetary reason more than proportional to the "heaviness" of the new currency, with exceptional cases tax.

[18] That instead according to the intuition of Carmelo Ottaviano, it should be called "ideaism" instead of "Idealism."

[19] Report on the P-2 Lodge by Tina Anselmi, chairman of the Parliamentary Commission of Inquiry.

[20] See Auriti, Application of a utility theory to a theory of law and the legal person, Att. II, Cong.
Nat. Fil. of Dir, Milan, 1956, p. 17 et seq.

[21] Ezra Pound, see above, p. 49.
[22] A closer look also the theft is none other than a withdrawal without consideration.
[23] See what was said about the monetary rarity, paragraph 13.
[24] See footnote 16, par. 17.

www.ingramcontent.com/pod-product-compliance
Lightning Source LLC
Chambersburg PA
CBHW072257170526
45158CB00003BA/1091